ISBN: 978-1-8382175-1-8

Dedicated to my Dad, Terry, who always said that some rules are meant to be broken. Just not these ones, though!

20 RULES OF PR
AKA – HOW TO GET IT RIGHT AND NOT F*CK IT UP

WHO IS THE PR MASTERCOACH?

Sam Brown has been in the PR business for over two decades, clocking up well over 50,000 hours of experience. She started as a publicist, working with fashion, drinks and entertainment brands, before launching her own agency specialising in reaching youth audiences for consumer brands, events, charities and the public sector.

Over the years, Sam has been involved in many award wins, including Best New Agency (Uproar Communications), Best Youth Campaign (Home Office, anti-knife campaign), and Global Impact (Selfridges Project Ocean).

Sam is now an independent Creative Director, Campaign Director and PR Coach, with brands and PR agencies across the globe. From the glamour of London Fashion Week to muddy fields of music festivals, and from global causes to grass-root communities, she creates and runs campaigns that have real impact... and has a lot of fun doing it, too!

"I think all agency teams should read this manual as an essential no-nonsense reminder on doing media relations properly. Sam has a mountain of experience working for global consumer brands and agencies alike so she knows what she's talking about... she delivers these gold nuggets of wisdom about working in the industry from her usual upfront perspective and with impeccable comedic timing – enjoy!". Lydia Hoye, Managing Partner. Kazoo PR, London

"Sam is one of a kind. She knows her stuff and says it like it is and with charm and humour. She is a great teacher and I am so pleased that she has written this book. It will be perfect read for those entering the field, and those with more experience who could use a tune up on how to work smarter. We love working with her and having her nurture our teams because she understands how the media works and how the media and PR's can get the best out of each other to create long-term relationships." Gabrielle Shaw, Founder, Gabrielle Shaw Communication

CONTENTS

INTRODUCTION

20
RULES
OF PR
AKA How
to get it
right and
not f*ck
it up

INTRO

Ahhh, PR! The great art of promoting and protecting; of persuasion and influence; and of endorsement and recommendation.

We don't instruct journalists to write stories, we don't produce catchy ads, and we don't hand out free samples in the shopping centre. We do things that people don't see and make them do things they didn't realise they wanted to do. Like buy a certain product, or go to an event, or support a cause.

Simple, right? No? Well, it kind of is when you know how, and follow some simple rules. Let me explain.

I'm Sam Brown, and I am *The PR Mastercoach*. I'm based in London, UK, and I've got over 20 years of experience in PR across the globe. 20 years is – quite literally – ages! In those 20 years, I've seen, learned and used every trick in the PR book. So, I've decided to put them all into a book. This book!

I've worked with consumers brands like Match.com, Smirnoff, Gillette, Bombay Sapphire and Britvic.

I've worked with fashion and beauty brands like Selfridges, Levi's, TONI&GUY, P&G and London Fashion Week.

I've worked with entertainment brands including Glastonbury Festival, Eventbrite, One Love Festival, and Virgin Media.

I've worked with UK government departments like the Home Office, Met Police and the NHS.

I've worked with charities like Oxfam, Centrepoint and the Prince's Trust.

And many, many more. But this isn't a CV. It's an advice-column-come-tipsheet-come-rule book.

20 rules, from over two decades in the business, and tips from the media themselves on how to (and not to) get results. Use this advice and you can help shortcut yourself to PR success, whether you're making your way in the industry or doing your own PR. It doesn't matter where you are in the world, or what it is you want to get into the media, these rules help you get it there and not f*ck it up. You have my word.

Sam Brown
The PR Mastercoach

1. AUDIENCE AUDIENCE AUDIENCE

20
RULES
OF PR AKA How
to get it
right and
not f*ck
it up

AUDIENCE. AUDIENCE. AUDIENCE.

This is the ultimate start and endpoint for everything...
and I mean eeeeeeeverything!

Who are you talking to?

Where are they?

What are they into?

What are their needs?

Why would they be interested in what you've got to say?

Why *wouldn't* they be interested?

Who influences them?

What media are they consuming?

Where do they 'live' online?

Knowing your audience goes way deeper than the basic demographics of age, gender and location. You need to understand their 'why'... Why would they choose 'Product A' over 'Product B'? Why would they react to one thing, but not another? Ask them why, and keep asking. You'll often need to ask 'why' four or five times before you get to the real heart of the matter.

If you don't know this, do not pass go and do not collect £200. Get to know your audience and understand them before you even start to think about talking to them. Your audience should always be seated at the head of the table. Feed them and they will feed you!

NEEDS MUST

20 RULES OF PR

AKA How to get it right and not f*ck it up

NEEDS MUST

When this one clicked with me, it changed a lot about the way I thought about PR:

Journalists need you, as much as you need them.

The never-ending love-hate relationship between PRs and journalists boils down to this simple fact. They have pages and airtime to fill... you have the story and the content. They have strict editorial control... you want a story told your way.

The balance is sometimes very delicate, but when you understand that you BOTH have a job to do, you can get the best out of the relationship. Be nice. Play fair. Be clear. Learn to negotiate.

Sounds simple, right? You'd think so, but so many PRs get this wrong. Some are intimidated and scared to speak to media. Some are at the other end of the spectrum, and are too full of themselves and behave like the media owes them something. Yes, be confident... but don't be a dick.

Treat the media as your partner. Understand what the other needs, and try to fulfil that need. It's that simple.

3. FACETIME

**20
RULES
OF PR**

AKA How
to get it
right and
not f*ck
it up

FACETIME

As much as you can, meet up with your media contacts. Relationships are built face-to-face and not through a screen.

This comes with a warning: Don't suffocate them, don't waste their time and don't be a stalker. Use the opportunity to be helpful and get to know more about them and what they need.

And while we all love a lunch paid-on-expenses at a fancy restaurant, it's not always the best way. Deskside appointments or going for a coffee can be just as effective. Not only are they quicker (and cheaper!), they're a much less intimidating way of meeting up.

With media meetings, treat them like a first date. Know what you want to talk about and don't eek it out unnecessarily. Be nice and genuine, not fake and flakey.

Which brings us to...

4. PR NOT ER

20 RULES OF PR AKA How to get it right and not f*ck it up

PR NOT ER

There have been many times when a media contact has called me in an emergency saying 'Can you help me with this thing, it's urgent' and it's resulted in a great piece of coverage. It might have been replacing a story that's fallen through or locating a one-of-a-kind product sample, or getting a last-minute quote from a spokesperson.

There was one time that I got a call on a Saturday evening when I was in my dressing gown getting ready to go out. A contact at a national Sunday newspaper had a story pulled at the last minute, and they knew that I had a story ready to go. A couple of phone calls and emails later, and it was done. A full page of coverage with my story appeared the very next day.

Did the story deserve a full page in a national paper? No... but it got it.

You don't get those calls unless you're known to be reliable and helpful. If you can't help, be honest. If you can help, follow through. Good media relationships are built on this principle.

Be helpful and the goodness will come back to you, promise.

Which also brings us to...

5. DON'T LIE

20
RULES
OF PR AKA How
to get it
right and
not f*ck
it up

DON'T LIE

It should go without saying, but don't lie to the media or in the media. Not even a little bit. You're not doing anybody any favours. At the very least, you'll lose all-important trust, and at worst you'll be caught up in a massive tangled web that you – and your brand, your story or your product – can't escape.

The only exception to this is April Fool's Day, when anything goes and everything is expected to be a lie. But that's the *only time,* ok?

This rule reminds me of a time when I worked with an overly chatty PR who, when a journalist mentioned that she had 'knitted a scarf over the weekend', the PR told the journalist that her brand ambassador – a well-known TV actress – had also recently taken up knitting. She hadn't. In fact, she'd never picked up a knitting needle in her life. You can imagine the surprise when the interview day came around, and the journalist had brought along her knitting bag with spare needles in the hope that the actress would join in.

What the PR thought was a nonchalant throwaway comment, the journalist thought was a great story angle. Both of them looked and felt extremely stupid... And just imagine what the actress thought when she was handed a ball of wool and two needles halfway through the interview.

Needless to say, the 2-page feature was dramatically cut, and the actress rightfully complained to the brand that she was representing. All over a foolish comment about knitting. So, rather than get yourself into knots and loops, just don't lie in the first place. It really isn't worth it!

6. THE 5 P'S - PRIOR PREPARATION PREVENTS POOR (SPOKESPERSON) PERFORMANCE

THE 5 P'S

Make sure spokespeople are fully briefed, so there's no risk of them saying anything stupid or going off-brand.

If you can't (or don't have the time or money to) put spokespeople through media training, have a think about what may come up and practise questions with your spokesperson. You may feel a bit silly pretending to be an interviewer, but it's better to feel silly for 10 minutes than to have it all fall apart in 10 seconds.

It's very rare to get interview questions in advance, but you can take a good educated guess. Think about any potential curveballs, or off-topic questions relating to a current news story, and prepare a line to pull the interview back on track.

Take a look at how British rapper Dizzee Rascal refused to get drawn into talking about the Black Lives Matter movement when interviewed on live TV about a concert he was taking part in. It's worth watching just to see Piers Morgan being told off, but it's a real-life example of how on-track messaging can easily go off-track and then back on again, all in the space of a few minutes. View the clip at tinyurl.com/PreparePrepare.

Ask yourself:

What could possibly trip us up here?

What's the worst question that could be asked?

What's happening in the world that has got absolutely *nothing* to do with the interview subject, but may get brought up for the sake of 'additional content'?

Why is this spokesperson involved? Do they have a right to comment?

And if they don't get anything else across, what's the one thing you need people to know?

Prepare, prepare, prepare.... Or you will be in *despair, despair, despair.*

7. WHO YOU GONNA CALL

WHO YOU GONNA CALL

While we're on the subject of spokespeople, think about who can say what, and to what media. Let's look at the example of the Dizzee Rascal drive-in concert announcement story again.

The artist himself was used to discuss the event on an entertainment slot on mainstream TV, as well as in music and what's on media.

The CEO of the concert production company may have made comments in the trade media on why the event was created.

The organisers could have been interviewed in the local media about why the event is taking place in their locality.

And on the day, concert goers (or some 'pre-selected superfans') may be asked for their opinions by a reviewer covering the event.

Four different people, four different viewpoints, four different stories, four different sections of the media. Look at how you can get more out of one story through the people who are involved.

8. THE HOOK (PART 1)

20
RULES
OF PR
AKA How
to get it
right and
not f*ck
it up

THE HOOK
(PART 1)

When emailing the media, make the hook of the story very clear from the very start - I cannot stress this enough!

You've got one line to hook the journalist in... ONE LINE... so don't waste it on any of that boring stuff that doesn't matter, especially if you're thinking 'oh, I should include it because of blah blah blah...'... No!

They don't want your life story, they want a headline, so think like them and it will make your life much easier. It doesn't matter whether you're pitching to a daily newspaper or a monthly lifestyle magazine, get your headline in place.

When you've written the headline, put it in the 'subject line' of the email. Not buried in the middle... not dumped at the end... put it top, front and centre. You don't go fishing with your bait halfway up your fishing line, do you? Then don't bury your bait!

9. ELEVATOR PITCH
(THE HOOK PART 2)

20
RULES
OF PR AKA How
to get it
right and
not f*ck
it up

ELEVATOR PITCH
(THE HOOK PART 2)

Yes, it's a cliché, but it's also very true. If you can't get your story across in the time it takes you to go up 3 floors in an elevator, you need to have a rethink. You are not JK Rowling, and you are not writing the next instalment to Harry Potter.

Show the journalist how you can fill their space with your story. Getting your point across in the neatest way possible is a craft. Learn how to do that, and you're much more likely to get listened to.

Once you've got your headline (front and centre, remember!?), strip your story back to the core details and put it into a few bullet-points. Be brief and be clear. Make it easy for the journalist to understand your story quickly, and they're more likely to say yes.

Literally - what's the story, why does it matter, what can you offer. Done.

And while we're on the subject of emails... for the love of god, please do not send over huge files and multiple attachments. Not only do the media not have the time to look at your 'encyclopaedia of information', most of them are receiving hundreds and hundreds of emails a day. Can you even imagine what a 30mb email will do to their inbox? Show some respect.

10. CALENDAR DAYS

20
RULES
OF PR AKA How
to get it
right and
not f*ck
it up

CALENDAR DAYS

There are so many 'National Something Days' or 'International Something Months', and not all are made equal.

In my time, I've created works of art out of pies for National Pie Week, created a song out of household items for Make Music Day, and taken a dwarf cupid into breakfast radio shows to read innuendo-filled poetry live on-air for Valentine's Day (please don't ask... it was a very different time...).

My point is, calendar days can be fun, or they can be thought provoking, or sometimes they can just be a useless hook that absolutely nobody cares about. Don't try and wedge your brand or product into something that doesn't connect.

When it comes to calendar days, choose them and use them wisely.

And while we're on the subject...

11. AUTHENTICITY RULES

20 RULES OF PR

AKA How
to get it
right and
not f*ck
it up

AUTHENTICITY RULES

Honestly, this rule is so important it should be written in capital letters, in bold, in italics, and then underlined...

Do not jump onto any political cause, movement, cultural celebration, religious festival or *anything similar* if it's not genuine and truly authentic. Is that clear?

There are zero exceptions to this rule.

Can you justify supporting the cause?

Do you have a right to be in that space?

Are you giving back, either financially or through action?

Does your audience even care?

Think hard and tread sensitively.

We are in an age where people and brands are regularly called out on fakery and lack of authenticity, and the backlash can be very damaging.

Don't be an invader and don't be tokenistic. Don't turn compassion on and off whenever you feel like it. Be real.

Now, go back and read this rule again because it needs to sink in. Unless, of course, you fancy putting a crisis comms plan into action... in which case, feel free to jump onto any bandwagon that comes along*. Cool?

*To be clear, that's sarcasm. Don't jump on any bandwagons

12. **SPEEDY DOES IT**

**20
RULES
OF PR** AKA How
to get it
right and
not f*ck
it up

SPEEDY DOES IT

Have you got any idea of the speed that journalists have to work?

Their deadlines are very hard and very fast. Rumour has it that Usain Bolt's trainer is an ex-news journalist*. Don't waste their time. If they ask you for something, respond promptly.

Get them what they need, as soon as you can possibly get it. Nobody is going to wait for you. You're not that important and there's likely to be someone, somewhere – possibly your direct competition - who can fill the request before you do. Be fast off the blocks.

*Another asterisk to confirm that this is obviously a fake-fact. It's not true but it serves the purpose to illustrate the point!

13.

EARLY BIRD CATCHES THE COVERAGE

**20
RULES
OF PR** AKA How
to get it
right and
not f*ck
it up

EARLY BIRD CATCHES THE COVERAGE

In the same vein, get information to the media as early as you can. There is a lot of competition for editorial space, so the earlier you stake a claim on a spot, the better.

Monthly and weekly titles plan their content well in advance. Monthly magazines, for instance, start work on their Christmas issues in July. They start to talk about this year's 'must have Christmas gift' when the sun's shining and they're wearing flip flops / thongs / sandals (depending on your location!).

Forward planners and researchers are your friends here. Let them know that the story is coming and when, even if the 'first alert' is just the top-line information. Ask them what they are working on and what their deadlines are. They're not monsters, they will tell you!

Think about any key dates that your feature authentically ties into, and flag these up. There may be other stories that other people, PR's and brands are putting forward that connect with what you're offering, and together, they could create a bigger feature. The easier it is for the journalist to make the connection, the better.

14. REMEMBER, REMEMBER

20
RULES
OF PR

AKA How
to get it
right and
not f*ck
it up

REMEMBER, REMEMBER

Whether you're speaking to multiple media contacts, or just one or two, keep track of your conversations. A simple spreadsheet will do the job.

If a media contact tells you an insight, note it.

If they ask you to follow up in two weeks' time, note it.

If they mention that there's a new section launching, note it.

It's hard enough to actually get to speak to journalists, so when you do, don't forget what they tell you!

15. READ THE ROOM

20
RULES
OF PR AKA How
to get it
right and
not f*ck
it up

READ THE ROOM

The tone that you approach the media with should suit the media outlet that you're speaking to.

If you're speaking to a youth title, a little slang and cultural references are fine, so long as they're authentic **(see Rule 11!)**.

If you're speaking to a trade title, however, you need a more professional tone and hard facts. Have stats at the ready.

Local newspapers can be approached a little more informally than a national broadsheet, and they appreciate you knowing the exact region that their outlet covers.

Read the room and play to it.

16. GET ON THE LEVEL

20
RULES
OF PR

AKA How
to get it
right and
not f*ck
it up

GET ON THE LEVEL

One of the biggest complaints from the media is about PRs contacting the wrong person, or contacting people at the wrong level. Learn what each person does and target the right one. If you don't know – just ask. Switchboard operators are particularly useful here, and they can also help on the correct pronunciation of an unusual name (very handy!).

As a general overview:

Editor of the publication – looks after the big picture for the whole publication, whether that's a website, a newspaper or magazine, and has overall control of content. The editor manages each of the section editors to create a cohesive issue. Do not pitch stories to this person!

Editor of the section, e.g. fashion editor, business editor, tech editor – oversees their specific pages or segment of a broadcast programme. They commission content, manage and control the workload of the team, and bring in contributors. In broadcast, they can be called editors or producers, depending on the outlet. This person can be pitched to.

Writer / Researcher / Assistant – co-ordinates and creates the content, and helps to bring the vision of the section editor to life. This person can be pitched to, but the decision to include a story will be made by their section editor.

This is obviously a very general overview and all media outlets vary slightly. The lower down the line you go the easier the contacts are to access, and the easier they are to get information from. Don't go in at the top unless you have something HUGE.

Remember that the assistants of today are the editors of tomorrow, so build relationships at that level and you will have the contacts that can be nurtured for years. The very best relationships between PRs and media are formed this way.

17. KNOWLEDGE IS KING

20
RULES
OF PR   AKA How
        to get it
        right and
        not f*ck
        it up

KNOWLEDGE IS KING

You know those annoying phone calls asking if you've been in an accident over the past three years? That's what it's like for journalists when you're trying to pitch a story that's not relevant to them. Useless, annoying and time wasting.

The way to real success is knowledge.

Knowledge of your audience and why the story is relevant to them.

Knowledge of the story and how you can carve it up into different angles for different media

Knowledge of the media outlet and what they're looking for to fill their space

Knowledge of the journalist and the type of story they cover.

It's this knowledge that sorts the good PRs from the not-so-good and the downright awful.

It's a skill, a craft and a science in equal measure, and there are no short cuts. Just do your research.

18. GO SOCIAL

20
RULES
OF PR **AKA How to get it right and not f*ck it up**

GO SOCIAL

Once you've identified your ideal media contact, look them up on social media. Specifically head to Twitter and Instagram, and give them a follow if relevant. This isn't about stalking – obviously – but their channels will give you lots of clues to what they're interested in **(see 'Knowledge is King' above!)**.

Many journalists regularly call-out on social media for contributions to features that they're working on. If you see something relevant, follow up fast as the opportunity will often be fulfilled very quickly.

Facebook is usually reserved as a personal online space, so rather than befriending a journalist on there, have a look for Facebook groups where journalists connect with PRs and brands. Groups such as FeatureMe!, where journalists working on national magazines and newspapers look for case studies, or Charity Marketing Network, where PRs in the not-for-profit and charity sector share tips and insights. Have a look to see what's relevant for your sector and region.

19. WORD ALERT !

**20
RULES
OF PR** AKA How
to get it
right and
not f*ck
it up

WORD ALERT !

Make sure you don't miss out on any mentions of you in the media – or mentions of your competitors – by signing up for free email alerts from services like Talkwalker and Google Alerts. These services automatically monitor your selected keywords across the internet, including news platforms, blogs, forums, websites and Twitter, and send you one email with everything collated.

There are a few ways to use these alerts, depending on how many emails you can cope with in your inbox:

First, monitor yourself, for obvious reasons.

Next, monitor your competition. With this, you can keep an eye on what they're up to, and also to check on where they're being featured that you're not.

Finally, you can monitor your keywords to see what's being discussed and who is discussing it. This can introduce you to new media targets to reach out to, and new opportunities for coverage. And it's all for free.

20. ...AND, THANK YOU

**20
RULES
OF PR**
AKA How
to get it
right and
not f*ck
it up

...AND, THANK YOU

Is it too hard to say thank you?

When a journalist writes something good about you, have the basic decency to thank them for it. The size of the thanks is up to you, but an email, a call, or repost and tag will suffice.

If understanding your audience is the ultimate starting point (*see Rule No1!*), then saying thank you is the ultimate finish.

Thanks and graciousness never goes unmissed, and are never forgotten. Which means that you won't be forgotten.

Remember that.

TIPS FROM THE MEDIA

I reached out to a few of my own media contacts and asked them one question: What tip would you give to PRs?

All of these words are straight from the horse's mouth – if horses were world class media, that is! There are some issues that come up again and again, as well as repeated mistakes that are easy to avoid.

So, if you don't want to be put on the black list, sent to the deleted items folder, or just don't want to f*ck it up, please heed these words of advice.

Jasmine Dotiwala – Multimedia broadcaster and journalist

IT'S A STORY NOT AN AD

Please respect that a journo's job is NOT to do PR but to find interesting stories. Do not insist on 'exact words, script or messaging'. Our editors see through this and will simply scrap the story if it reads like an advert. Do give us a variety of angles on your client/story. Always answer why this is a unique story which would be of wider interest to a niche or broad audience.

Please don't promise us an exclusive then give it to someone else. That's automatic blacklist action! And remember that everything you say is ON THE RECORD unless you say otherwise. Don't fly into a frenzy when something you shared is out in the public if you didn't specify it was OFF THE RECORD.

Daniela Soave – Culture journalist and editor

WHO YOU REACH OUT TO

Do your research on who you're pitching to. Is your product/event relevant to their publication? Does the journalist cover that particular area? And, most importantly, make sure you spell their name correctly if you are writing to them personally.

Oliver Poole – Independent and Evening Standard journalist

HIT THE DESK AT THE RIGHT TIME

The crucial thing is to know what time to call. Catch a reporter ahead of that outlet's daily editorial news conference, when they are desperately looking for something to tell their editor so they have something to add to the news list, and they will be much more likely to pitch it to desk as it makes them look like they are on top of their brief.

Laura Lee Davis – Arts, parenting and lifestyle journalist and former editor of Time Out London

MANAGING COPY APPROVAL

As a writer and editor, if I am asked for copy approval, I would point out that it would makes us both look bad. If the PR is worried about what I am going to do to their client, perhaps they should think again about working with my publication or website. If this doesn't stick and the PR still needs something to go back to the agent or client with, I would suggest quote approval – after all, I don't want to misquote someone. Once or twice pop stars have demanded that they recorded the interview as well as me. This is fine, I've had the luxury of working for publications that are not going to demand I make up anything scurrilous. And who wants to end up in court?! (On my favourite occasion, a big actor pulled out his tape recorder and mine totally outclassed his, but hey, size doesn't matter...). Always remember that a friendly chat can come up with a good two-way solution, and everyone's happy. Please don't demand.

Antony Baxter – News Editor, London Live

DON'T BLANKET

Avoid the blanket approach, and make sure it is relevant to the organisation you're emailing. I often receive press releases with "we hope your readers will be interested in hearing about… or we'd love it if you could include x in your next article". That's a turn off for me, and puts the press release to the back of the list for those I take seriously. What works for print doesn't always work for broadcast media, which has specific visual requirements.

Secondly, and perhaps more important, is to consider the different rules between broadcast news programmes and print. I get dozens of press releases a week asking to feature a specific product, a new drink, a new club, a new type of chocolate etc. Because of rules around product placement within news programmes, there's very little we can do with these - so make sure you target the right company, or the right part of a company. Commercial channels like London Live survive on advertising, they never, and can't let it slip through for free in a news feature, but they'll be happy to discuss an ad slot with you.

Hannah Fernando, Group Celebrity Director, Future Plc (inc. Marie Claire, Now Celebs, Chat, Woman, Woman's Weekly)

DO YOUR HOMEWORK

This is my biggest piece of advice - I am not called Anna or Hanna or even Helen, I am Hannah. I do not work in finance nor sales - so does your e-mail apply to me? Am I really the best person to speak to and why? If you pass this test then fire the email at me and I WILL respond. Making sure e-mails are tailored to the person you are sending it to is key, despite the fact that you may have a generic e-mail message that has to go to a number of different people. Less is more inthis case. A scattergun approach will not reap the best reward in my opinion. In a world where people are stretched and time is a luxury, emails that have no bearing on a job will likely be deleted.

Ed Cumming – freelance writer, Observer, Telegraph, Vogue

KEEP IT PERSONAL

My advice would be to keep things as personal as possible. Clearly this won't apply to every area but it's best when a PR has taken the time to think about who you are and what you do, and then comes with an idea that is tailored accordingly.

Michael Thomas, CLASH Magazine and co-founder of Ourhood Community

KNOW THE CULTURE

There is nothing better than a PR that knows your business, your wants and needs. Sending over relevant stories is so important for both parties. If done right it makes people look forward to receiving your emails and saves everyone time. It's always appreciated when PRs take the time to read the magazine and website and understand our culture.

Nesha Fleischer – Time Out London

WORK TOGETHER

Keep it simple and know your audience. Always try to find a creative angle, and above all, be flexible. We're all in this together.

Paloma Lacy – food writer, South London Press, London Weekly News

GET TO KNOW ME

I've bounced between journalism and PR for a very long time. I know how hard both jobs are, despite the general public's preconception. I conclude the PRs' lot is a tougher gig – difficult clients are far worse than the toughest editors. PRs, please send me any information that you think I may be interested in. I hold no truck with journalists complaining about emails sent – if it's irrelevant, I'll press delete. Even if this is the case, I'll generally respond to those I know well and simply say it's not for me.

Just one small request, please get my name right. It isn't Pamela or Pavlova but Paloma. This is the best way to begin a bad conversation. If I come across a name I'm unfamiliar with, I simply ask for a steer.

Lee Tyler – editor, Blues & Soul Magazine

WHO & WHEN

Leave at least 72 hours before you follow up your initial pitch. If possible, do not to send emails that start with just "Hi". Find out who the correct contact is. Start by checking the internet and social media for this information. How you treat your client or your brand is exactly how you treat the titles you pitch to… remember, no matter who your client is, we do not owe coverage to anyone.

Ask the title for both deadline and shelf dates in advance, a launch date that misses both would explain why your initial pitch may not have been replied to and will save you time with repeatedfollow-ups. Be aware of a title's policy regarding advertising, in recent years a pay-to-play policy has been adopted by many magazines and websites.

Holly Buckley – editor, fashion trade bible Diary Directory

BE RELEVANT

We have the same feedback regularly from our media partners. When the media make a specific request, PRs send over everything they have, whether it's relevant or not. This just lowers the effectiveness of the call-out for everyone. Be selective in what you send, and answer the specific request the media has made.

The PR Mastercoach is a training and mentoring program developed by PR pro Sam Brown. The program includes this book, online training courses, face-to-face coaching, and an Instagram channel for regular PR tips and inspiration. Find out more at **ThePRMastercoach.com**.